I0559243

HOW TO MARKET A BOOK SOMEONE BESIDES YOUR MOTHER WILL READ

By

Tierney James

How To Market A Book Someone Besides Your Mother Will Read ©2018 by Tierney James

Cover design and formatting by
Sweet 'N Spicy Designs

P R E S S

Owasso, OK

ISBN - 978-1-965460-16-0 (Paperback)
ISNB - 978-1-965460-17-7 (eBook)

Dedication

To a fellow author, Shirley McCann. She never fails to make me look good on social media. Thank you for your constant support and encouragement.

Table of Contents

It All Began with a Puppet Play

From the time I was ten years old and wrote my first puppet play, I knew writing stories, novels, and plays was a magical life. Discovering I could create characters, worlds, and adventure, gave my parents more reason to wonder what was wrong with me. I wrote pages and pages, of what I know now, was nonsense with tons of spelling and grammatical errors. Those stories found their way into a discarded Avon box I kept in the closet. My best friend adored my stories and read them like I had written *Gone with the Wind.* It was enough to keep me scribbling in notebooks every chance I got.

A wonderful thing happened in the ninth grade when my English teacher read my short story to the class and announced I was a writer. At the time I thought I'd finally made it in the literary world. Probably not important that my story was less than five hundred words on wide ruled paper or that my character, a peeping tom, turned out to be a black cat. No matter what I wrote the English teachers and librarians wanted to read it. I nearly broke my arm patting myself on the back.

Then I switched schools. My sophomore English teacher was not impressed. As a matter of fact, my first writing assignment looked like a crime scene with red marks splashed top to bottom. Had she cut her hand while grading? Then I saw my grade; C+. No matter what I wrote for this teacher, it never received glowing comments, encouragement to press on or that I had a future in journalism. But I learned a valuable lesson; not everyone would like what I wrote. Sometimes I will have to work harder to get the attention I want and maybe deserve.

Over the years I continued to write and hide the words in notebooks or in boxes under the bed. My confidence dwindled but not my love of writing. There did come a time when I had to choose to be a full time participating mom or write. Back then computers were not in every home office and that electric typewriter left a lot to be desired when it came to corrections and edits. Working full time as a teacher made it possible to still be with my kids in our rural school system while I worked on my Masters of Education degree. Writing became a distant dream.

When my youngest prepared to go off to her first year in college, she made me promise I would start my writing career. By that time my writing ability, or so I thought, resembled a rusty nail. Several more years passed before I decided to give it a try. I met a lovely lady who had published several creative non-fiction books and she suggested we meet and share words.

To say I was terrified might be an understatement. With a great deal of trepidation, I emailed her the first few pages of a story about my mother. When we met for coffee later in the week, I remembered my high school English teacher who was so hard on me. Then the magical words flowed from her mouth, "My goodness. I didn't know what to expect, but you're a real writer."

Ancient history now. That was all I needed to start writing full time. One thing I wasn't prepared for, though, was how to market myself and my work. Writing the story is only half the job. I failed miserably in branding myself and preparing for what happens when you write the words, "the end." No one was there to show me how. I spent the next four years learning the ropes of marketing. I'm still trying new things as I go along.

Why write this book? I want to share my marketing plan for new authors, beginning writers, and for dreamers who stare at notebooks and journals and long to make words into magic. You need to start your marketing plan from the moment you write your first paragraph.

Not all of the hints, advice or plans I offer will work for you, but some will. There won't be time to do all of them, but you'll have time to try many of these ideas. Some are more involved than others, but after you implement a few things, it will become easier. Don't be afraid. You can do this. Take it from a shy, nerdy girl, who wanted to be a war correspondent, an astronaut and teacher, you just have to try.

Author Branding

"I haven't even finished my first book (story). Why do I need to start marketing?" Sound familiar?

Reinventing the Wheel – YOU!

Check out this article by Writer's Relief Staff: http://www.huffingtonpost.com/2014/04/30writing

"You spend your days and nights writing, rewriting, and submitting your work to literary agents or journals. That's everything a "hoping-to-be-successful" writer needs to do, right? Not quite. In today's media-savvy publishing industry, it's just as important for writers to develop their author brands."

Most of us know what kind of story we plan to write. If we didn't, the first paragraph would never get written. In my case, I knew because there are certain genres of stories I like to read and even more that interest me. There are authors I love and never bother to read the book jacket before purchasing. I see their name and I'm pulling out the credit card. James Rollins, Vince Flynn, Brad Thor, Steve Berry, Sandra Brown and Nora Roberts don't have to work at getting me to buy their books. Their branding of what and how they write won me over a long time ago.

But I'm here to tell you, if I picked up a book with Brad Thor's name boldly written on the front and it turned out to be a Nicolas Sparks type romance, I'd have a meltdown. Or if Jane Yolen wrote a Stephen King type children's book, I probably wouldn't buy another one of her books. (You might hear the Twilight Zone theme song here.)

To put it another way, let's go the movies. If you were to buy a ticket to a Melissa McCarthy and Will Ferrell movie, thinking your funny bone was about to be tickled, then discovered it concerned drug addicts who beat their kids, wouldn't you demand your money back? Run through the movies you like to watch. Does a theme emerge? Are you ever disappointed? Why?

Building a brand is a matter of trust, a contract you make with readers. When you switch gears, you run the risk of losing your fans. From project to project, maintaining style, voice, genre, and pace becomes a safety net for your readers. They depend on you for consistency.

The Huffington Post link I included suggested you "Find your voice and be consistent in your writing. Book cover design is a great place to display your author branding." A book series has something similar on each cover. Even before the book jacket is opened, your reader knows it is you. I learned this the hard way and ended up redoing my covers for the Enigma Series.

"Remember: A clear, consistent author brand can make the difference between writing as a hobby and writing as a career."

Branding – Ideas

1. Make a list of authors you like - Evaluate their book jackets – What made you pick it up the first time? Color, lettering, blurb, picture, size, category?

2. Decide your niche or genre – It's okay to have several as long as there is something that connects them. I like to write geopolitical thrillers. I also like to write science fiction thrillers and paranormal thrillers. Romantic suspense is also in the mix. My conceptional vision for them are action/adventure or edge of your seat complications. There is always a "thriller" edge to them.

3. Who is your audience?

4. Will you have a pen name? That depends on you and your lifestyle. Do you want to keep part of your personal life private? Are you hiding from the Mafia?

Now that you've established the kind of stories you love and want to write, let's start developing a plan.

Website & Design

Marketing is a slippery slope for most of us. One piece of that puzzle is creating a website to help promote you, your work, and your wisdom. I tried Blogger for a few years, but I outgrew it. I tried making my own website. (Hilarious laughing here.) My search led me to Jennifer Davis of J Davis Web Design. By looking at other author websites and talking to them, I discovered I didn't have to go it alone.

Most of the time when Jennifer hears from me these days it's because I've screwed something up, scared I've been invaded by spam monsters or want to change something. Oh yeah. And I have deleted things where she had to swoop in and rescue my words. I'm a mess. And she is a goddess! Are you blushing, Jennifer?

Jennifer Davis jen@jdaviswebdesign.com is who I used for my website design. She was affordable. I checked around and some people want thousands to do this. The nice thing about Jennifer is when I screw up, she jumps in and fixes my mess. Lisa Ricard Claro is another author who used her. I love her site. Jennifer encourages you to look at all her designs before settling on just one.

WordPress and GoDaddy have avenues to create your own website. I'm sure there are others. I was pretty dense on trying to do this. It was worth the money and it is a tax write-off.

She is going to explain a few things to you now. Pay attention.

How can writers best use their website?

An author's website is the best place to house everything about an author's work:

- Showcase your in-progress and published books (with cover images, blurbs, buy links, and excerpts).
- Include a page that digs deeper into who you are as a person (hobbies? day job? favorite books or authors?).
- Provide an easy way for readers to contact you with a contact form.
- Interact and educate with blog posts (which can be automatically shared to your social media accounts, saving time).
- Link to your social media accounts (or even have social media posts or tweets displayed on your site in a sidebar).

Can authors create their own website themselves?

Yes! But you'll need time, a reasonable level of tech-savviness, patience, and most importantly, acceptance that you may not achieve the site of your dreams—in many cases, because the theme or template you chose has limitations—it simply wasn't designed with what you have in mind. Many of my clients previously created their own websites and either became frustrated with the complicated setup or found they couldn't achieve what they truly wanted with a stock theme; thus, they turned to me.

What pitfalls to watch out for when finding someone to create your website?

- Do not pay more than necessary. There is a wide range of pricing for web design, and I am stunned by what some designers charge for a simple information-only website. Ask around first.

- I've noticed a number of designers charging high-end prices to set up a website based on a commercially-available theme. While some of these themes can be complex (with oodles of options to wade through), why not pay less and have a custom theme that does exactly what you want?

- Be sure any designer you are considering has a portfolio of sites they can show you. Don't just look at pictures. Get the site links and look at the sites the designer has created. You want to be sure the designer can achieve the functionality you desire.

- Do not work with a designer who insists only THEY can make changes to your website. The entire point of a WordPress site is so you can maintain and update your site when you need to.

What are the steps to having a custom website created?

- First, I ask authors to view the sites I've designed (from both my client portfolio and my demo WordPress sites) and pick one to be a "starting point". This does not mean the author's website will look exactly like the chosen site, only that it gives me an idea of where to start with the custom design.

- In order to give the rock-bottom price, I charge authors, I don't create the page background or header illustrations. In terms of backgrounds, there are numerous free web backgrounds available online. A photo works well as a background too. The background can be overlaid with an opaque layer to ensure readability—such as with Tierney's website! Illustrations for the header can be purchased from any number of stock image sites for very reasonable prices. Some authors have chosen to have a "signature logo" created by a graphics designer, otherwise, I will use one of the many Photoshop fonts.

- Authors provide any photos they want to be used on the site. If the image desired was not purchased or labeled as free and reusable, be sure to obtain permission—do not simply take photos from the internet!

- Once authors have their hosting account and domain set up with a hosting company (see below on "Choosing a domain name and web host"), I install WordPress, the custom theme, all the necessary plugins, and set up the sidebars (there are many wonderful widgets available in WordPress).

- I create the Home Page, Contact page, Author Bio page, Books page, and blog. Additionally, I provide an instruction doc on how to use WordPress, as well as free email support. And all the WordPress sites I design are responsive (meaning they automatically adjust to be viewed on a desktop computer, smaller devices such as an iPad, and smartphones).

- If the author has an existing blog on WordPress.com or Blogger.com, I can import the blog posts into the new site. If the author's blog is on a different platform (e.g., Wix, Weebly), where the RSS feed can be exported, the blog posts can still be imported into the new WordPress site (albeit without images). There are additional options for importing sites created on other online platforms.

Choosing a domain name and web host.

To have a custom WordPress website, you will need a domain name and a hosting account. In terms of a domain name, most authors chose a domain that incorporates their author name. If your name is not unique, you might add "author" to the domain (such as janedoeauthor.com). As for hosting, I have found both Bluehost and GoDaddy to be easy to work with for both domain management and site hosting, but any major web host is fine (and by major, I mean, not a web server running in someone's basement). You want a hosting account where you have access to all the WordPress files both via a built-in File Manager from your hosting account and FTP. And don't worry—I can walk you through all the "techy" details.

How did you get started in web design?

I created my first website in 1996 for a research project while working on my master's thesis. I hadn't intended to be a web designer, but with every research project I worked on, I was asked to create an accompanying website. Word of mouth led to additional requests for my web work. Now I work from home where I spend half of my time on web design and the other half writing! I am a published romance author as well. I love that I have both the technical aspects of web programming and the creative outlet of writing.

Thank you so much, Jennifer, for giving us the skinny on website design. You can check out the website she created for me at tierneyjames.com I love it!

A website screams you're a professional. This is where you can blog, promote your favorite charity, post interviews, post upcoming events where your audience can come see you, share recipes and the list goes on. Maybe you restore old cars in your spare time. This is a great place to post those pictures. Basically, this is where readers can find out about you and that you are a living, breathing human being who in many ways, experiences the same challenges the non-writer does.

Give Back

You can use your website to help others. One of the things I did was write a children's book for Mission K9 Rescue which rehabilitates military dogs. All the proceeds of the book will go to them. Another tax write-off but that is not why I did it. I believed in the work they were doing. I feature them on my website too. I have a page just for worthy causes.

Benefits:

1. Share the love
2. Gets the attention of others you want to read your books
3. Good karma

Promote your ideals and beliefs without making a big deal about it.

Go Daddy

This is who hosts my website. You need this. There are others but Go Daddy seems to be the most experienced. They are also very willing to work with you when things go sideways. They offer domain names (which you must have) and it comes with an email address. You need an email with your name in it. tierneyjames.com is my address. My domain is Tierney James. When you put in Tierney James in your search engine I pop up everywhere. I also spring for tierneyjames.net. You can get a spam filter so you don't get ridiculous ads or inquiries. My website designer has my info so if I screw something up or get a weird note she goes in and sees what is going on. Several times she has told me to contact GoDaddy because someone was trying to sell me items under their name. They also notify you when it is time to renew.

Newsletter

Is this important? I used to tell people "Not if you're just starting out. But I'm four years into this so it is time I take the plunge." USA Best Selling Author, Cara Bristol, has a newsletter that comes out about once a month. In hers, she showcases her WIP (work in progress), backlist books, contests and much more. She started out small with MailChimp. Remember it is free for the first 2000 or so subscribers. She is way past that now. Impressive. Cara believes it is never too soon to start your newsletter. Here are some excellent reasons to take this next step.

- **Target marketing** – People who are interested in your work or is a fan from the get-go will love getting updates on new releases, event dates, and contests.

- **Develops a relationship**

- **Rewards for fans** – Newsletters can offer your fan base coupons, special offers, and "sneak peeks" of your WIP.

- **Brief article** – Pack it full of helpful hints on a topic which might relate to your next book or blog post. It's not all about you!

- **Elements of grace and mercy** – Offer resources where your reader can get more information about a topic. AGAIN! It's not all about you. Helping others is just good karma and good business.

- **Testimonials** – I'm here to tell you if Steve Berry ever writes the words, "Great read" to me I'm going to be waving it on a flag in my front yard. Don't be afraid to share those moments of praise from someone who thinks you're special. Maybe it won't be Stephen King, but it might be a soldier who read your piece on the Korean War or a local chef who loved your cookbook.

- **Contact** – Just like in your media kit, you need to provide the best way to contact you. Some authors give out their phone numbers and home address. I don't. When you write thrillers, you stay in a constant state of paranoia.

- **Good graphics** – Because I'm a visual learner, I like pretty things. Pictures capture my attention on a piece of paper before anything else. I bet most of us are like that. There is no excuse not to use your photos, memes, and other free outlets to put a little sparkle or intrigue into your newsletter.

- **Be clever** – Using a famous quote or joke, is food for the soul. Maybe you have a faith-based newsletter; then use scripture or share a close encounter with someone who made you believe in miracles. Add a favorite recipe or travel tip. The sky is the limit.

Here are some places to get started on your newsletter.

1. MailChimp www.mailchimp.com/ is the world's leading email marketing platform. 15 million customers, from small e-commerce shops to big online retailers, use MailChimp to express themselves to the world.

2. Constant Contact www.constantcontact.com/

3. How to Make a Newsletter | Lucidpress**https://www.lucidpress.com/pages/how-to-make-a-newsletter** The details of a newsletter will depend on its audience. Above all, newsletters should be informative and add value for readers.

Microsoft Word Newsletter - How to Create a Newsletter Using Microsoft Word Video - YouTube https://www.youtube.com/watch?v=tWXbrWpwpSw Uploaded by Johnny Rogers. Visit http://www.JohnzPChut.com/ -- Not sure how to set up and **create a newsletter** in Microsoft Word 2007 ... I did not do this. But it's out there if you need it.

Navigating Social Media & How It Works for You

Many new authors don't realize that when they send a manuscript to a publisher they want to know your online presence. They may even go online and look for you if you have sparked an interest. If they can't find you, then they may not be interested.

Decadent Publishing put a policy in place to encourage new authors to carve out a niche for themselves on social media. Other publishers, if interested in your manuscript may give you six months to establish your brand. When I signed on with Black Opal Books a number of years ago, the contract clearly stated I would be responsible for a certain amount of the marketing.

 If you only want to sell to your family and a few friends then don't bother with this section. But I have to tell you when someone in Upper Sandusky, Ohio goes on Facebook and recommends my book, I'm pretty pumped!

I have writer friends and fans all over the world that find my work. To tell you the truth, after the first book, my family wasn't all that interested in reading my stories. They don't even buy them and often expect me to give them a copy.

Who am I kidding? They know the author's PROOF, casually laying on top of some books on the coffee table, can be borrowed at any time. The really lame thing I do is nudge it their way. Then someone turns to the window and shouts, "Look, Haley's Comet!" The book doesn't move much.

My experience has been when you sign with a traditional publisher, they expect you to do between 75%-90% of the marketing while they move on to the next project. So, whether you are an indie author or a traditional author, the work is the same.

There are many social media outlets, but this is a good start for today. If you don't know what this is, then we need to catch you up to the here and now.

1. **Pinteres**t – Users "pin" images that they find on the web to virtual pinboards. You don't have to write much. Speaks for itself. www.pinterest.com/ptierneyjames/ is my site. This is a great place to let people know who you are, your likes, dislikes, your books, showcase other people, TV shows, keep ideas for future projects (keep those secret) and even writing advice.

2. **Facebook** – https://www.facebook.com/TierneyJames1/ is my author page, not my regular page. This again tells something about me but not necessarily about my books. You can also post events, share updates, and exchange ideas. Make it more than just about your books. Otherwise, it looks like

you're screaming "BUY ME" all the time. People click on your account because they want to know more about you.

3. **Tumblr** – You create a Tumblelog where you can publish short posts of text, images, quotes, links, video, audio and chats. You can link your Tumblr account to other social networks you use as well. For more information go to https://www.lifewire.com/tumblr-overview-for-bloggers-3476387

4. **Twitter** – Using 280 characters or less you create tweets or updates. The uses are all over the place. News, opinions, quotes, links, photos or just about anything. This is my go-to social media spot. I post every day, sometimes three or four times a day. Be sure to have a greater number of followers than you follow. I use pictures 99% of the time from my own files. Try not to just post BUY MY BOOK. Put in funny things about you, the news, your vacation, a blog link, or an upcoming event like GOT MARKETING! I also do a thing called RETWEET TUESDAY.

- On retweet Tuesday I look back over the last week's notifications. Whoever has loved or retweeted me then I do the same for them. I also will go to my followers and choose a few people to retweet I haven't heard from in a while. This comes back to me tenfold and I usually get some new followers.

Twitter Tips

- 280 Characters

- Handle – TierneyJames1

- Hashtag (#amwriting)

- DM – Direct message

- RT – Retweet

- MT – Modified tweet

- Use @ when replying to another user.

- Shorten if possible

- Use www.bitly.com to shorten links

- Remember you're building relationships.

- Hootsuite can be used to schedule your tweets.

- Clean the slate at least once a month – If they haven't followed you, delete them.

5. **Google+** – Another networking platform – Circles and hangouts are created that have similar interests to yours. To find out more go to whatis.techtarget.com/definition/Google-plus.

6. **YouTube** – This is a website where you can share or watch a video. I also use it to listen to music while I write. I repost some of what I see on my Twitter and Facebook accounts.

7. **Instagram** – If your kids haven't already told you, this is a mobile photo-sharing series that allows you to share pictures, videos to all kinds of platforms such as Facebook, Twitter, Tumblr, and Flickr.

What happens when you use social media?

1. It will refer traffic to your blog, website, the landing page for your books, and Amazon.

2. There is a large community of indie authors who are willing to help you promote your book and form supportive alliances. Even if you're not an indie author, writing groups, clubs, and friends, are all on social media and will give you a shout out when you need it.

3. You'll find new readers on social media.

4. Social media helps you to market your books.

5. You can get to know professionals, who can show you how to improve your book marketing efforts, write better blog posts, tune up your author website, and more efficiently use social media. You can also meet editors, designers, book reviewers and bloggers, and publicists.

6. Over time, social media will help you to build your community.

7. You'll meet readers who can become your "Super Fans" or belong to your "Street Team."

8. When you host giveaways and contests, you'll need social media to spread the word.

9. With social media, you can inform your followers and readers about new blog posts you write. You can also recommend books fairs, movies, and your favorite reads.

10. Social media will allow you to build relationships with your readers.

You can sell to a worldwide audience. I have followers on several continents. How cool is that?

Creating the Meme – What is it and why it's important?

When you create a meme for social media or online party it adds a freshness to the cover of your book. If people see the same book cover over and over it becomes invisible. I use these on Twitter, Facebook, and Tumblr. Same book. Different face. I also use these as writing prompts or questions when I do a release party. I've made a variety of these for different holidays like Christmas. I save them and use them next year. If you know your story already, you can start creating. Most of them are free.

1. Canva.com

2. Free Photos – Shutterstock, Flotilla

3. Affordable backgrounds you can find on the floor or in the walls.

4. Let's create a meme

    - Go to canva.com

    - Set up an account

    - Log in

    - Choose something from "Create a Design". I suggest for this we use the Social Media item. It's the first one and you'll probably use it the most.

    - Choose your background. Remember to choose things that are free.

- On the left, there are other details you'll want to explore. They are pretty explanatory. Again. Choose the free items. Click on your choices and they should appear on your Social Media screen. I also upload pictures of my book covers, designs I've photographed (like rugs, wall textures, etc.) to upload.

- After you have just what you want you'll be able to download it to your computer. If you've chosen something with a price, then you'll have to pay at this time. Avoid doing that if possible.

Here are a few of my creations.

Check out my other social media sites to see how I created headers. I change these up every few months to keep things fresh. I also use memes when I'm posting on Facebook groups where readers visit. This is an opportunity for them to give your book a second look. Not too long ago I saw where a reader purchased my book just because of the teaser on the meme.

Media Kit – Create it!

In Joan Stewart's writing tips, she says "Your book's media kit is the major marketing package that tells a variety of audiences about the book and makes it easy for them to report on it or promote it.

Yet many authors are confused about what goes into the kit. If you've written more than one book, you should have one media kit for each book. But some of the materials in all those media kits can be the same, such as your author bio." Let's start now.

Author Bio

Include a series of four bios, written in different lengths to make the media's job easy. You do not want journalists and others who need just a short paragraph about you to pick and choose from the information you provide in one epic bio. They just don't have the time to wade through your clever life, so make it easy for them. Besides, there's no guarantee what they write will be accurate. Include an "Author Bio" sheet with bios, all written in the third person, in these four sizes. This is something you can include in each of your kits you create for your novels.

- **Two-line bio.** This should be 140 characters which used to be what Twitter allowed. Why so short? Because if someone wants to tweet a description about you, you've already written it. Magazines often provide a resource box where space is tight. Make it fit.

- **Short bio** (50 words). This is ideal for longer author resource boxes. Focus on your expertise, not your book. Did you work for NASA? Know how to hunt alligators for dinner?

- **Medium bio** (100 words). Include everything in the short bio. Include your most noteworthy accomplishments.

- **Long bio** (400 to 600 words). Write an overview of your life and writing career. Include everything in the medium bio. You can use this to tell a story but keep it simple.

- **Speaker introduction.** This is very helpful for meeting organizers and others who invite you to speak. Never let them write your introduction. Insist that they read the one you provide. Write up to 300 words. Don't let them pick and choose what they deem important.

- **Fun facts you didn't know about me.** I love this part. These can include trivia from your personal or writer's life, unusual hobbies or travels, or maybe a favorite recipe or tip, that will give readers a glimpse into your personality. Maybe you're a ghost hunter in your spare time. I used to be a Solar

System Ambassador for NASA's Jet Propulsion Lab. I also had the distinction of being part of the shuttle crew at Space Camp for Educators who left the cargo bay doors open. Our coach waited with a scowl on her face and announced we'd burned to a crisp on reentry. Yikes. Funny now. Not so much then.

Book Synopsis

I know what you're thinking. I hate to write these. Everyone hates them. Your book is done and you want to move on, not prepare something to excite yet another publisher or book market. This is helpful when you need a quick introduction to your work for radio or television. Write these all in the third person, in four different lengths: a two-line summary, short, medium and long. Take your time to consider the full scope or the big picture of the book before writing each synopsis.

Consider what the book has to offer, the most compelling parts of the story, or the niche the book serves. Write short and pointed sentences that are appropriate for a general audience and pitch your book in as few words as needed. Longer is not better.

2-line Summary: 140 characters

This short summary can be used with reviews or articles. Concentrate on your book's strongest storyline or marketing niche that will attract a reader. *"My Wild About Cooking"* book works perfectly for the outdoorsman in your life.

Short Synopsis: 50 words

This is ideal for the short caption or description that may accompany your book's cover picture on a website, blog, or bookstore window. Boil your work down to its most essential elements.

Medium Synopsis: 100 words

Include everything in the short synopsis, plus some added detail about the book's content or story. Do you read the backside of DVDs? That is what you're striving for to create a lasting impression. Crisp. Clean. To the point.

Long Synopsis: 400 to 600 words

In this longer synopsis give readers a good overview of the book, its storyline or its marketing niche. Is it horror, non-fiction, speculative fiction or something that is trending? A positive review or awards can be tacked onto the end.

Points of Interest in the Book's Content or Story

When I wrote *The Rescued Heart,* people were curious how I learned how to bring down a mine and rescue buried miners. Turns out my husband was a mine engineer who helped me write about explosives and other dangerous aspects of mining. I even took a class. I also wrote a children's book titled *There's a Superhero in the Library.* My school librarian friend battled breast cancer in such a fun and comical way she became my hero. I dedicated the book to her.

These may or may not get published. but at least you'll have them if space allows. Seeing the human side of you and your journey in writing a particular book fascinates people. Show how it is unique and how it may serve a particular audience. Will the book make a difference in someone's life? When you know someone with cancer, it just might.

I once received a phone call to meet reader at a McDonalds just off the interstate. They had heard about my children's book dealing with cancer and wanted to buy five for her aunts as Christmas gifts. And the book has a very happy ending! We talked about my hero and that cancer no longer was a death sentence. We parted friends and the books went to a deserving family.

Press Release Include contact information, a headline, and subhead. Start with the book and explain what the reader will learn. Sometimes your publisher will do this for you. I'm an indie author now but still have a team in place. My formatter/publisher is happy to write a press release on her stationery.

Include a quote from the author. It can include why you wrote the book, what you hope readers will learn or advice included in the book. Don't forget to include a link to your website or other outlets where readers can purchase your book.

Sample Chapter

Choose a chapter that reflects what the book is about. You can include a link to a Table of Contents and Amazon reviews. Some bloggers like to have this too if they feature you on their website.

Interview Questions

Do you ever wonder how most journalists and broadcasters have time to read a book then ask such interesting questions to the author? Surprise! They don't have time. Most may have only read the blurb or synopsis. Some of those books are five hundred pages long. That's why you need to prepare a list of interview questions. They won't necessarily limit the interview to those questions, but the list will provide a handy springboard that will help them start the conversation. And the upside is you'll already know the answers to the questions. A definite plus in my book. That is one place surprises aren't good.

Maybe a news outlet wants you to weigh in on a possible terrorist threat at a hospital because they have radioactive isotopes. As luck would have it you just wrote an action-adventure thriller where such a thing happened. You have lots of little tidbits of information in your head, so write those questions for the interviewer because it is possible they don't even know what an isotope is. But you do.

Interview Questions for (author's name)

> 1. Why did you write (book title)?
>
> 2. Was there any one person who was your inspiration for the main character (include his or her name)?
>
> 3. In the book, you say "(include a controversial or compelling statement or a key point)." Why do you feel that way?
>
> 4. What's the most important thing readers will learn from (book title)?
>
> 5. People listening to this often struggle with (problem). What's your best advice on how they can deal with that?
>
> 6. When do you write? Is it easier to write in the morning or at night?
>
> 7. Who's your favorite author**?**
>
> 8. Where can we buy the book?

Contact Information

Include a sheet that tells people how to contact you: it may be by office phone, email, Skype, etc. Be sure to add links to all your social media profiles. This may well be the most important item in your media kit. If you're mailing copies of your book to reviewers, it's a good idea to slip a copy of your press release and the contact information sheet into the book. Some authors include their home address. There have been a few times, if the situation dictates, I'll leave my cell phone number. I don't feel comfortable giving out too much information. If they have my email, I'm pretty much going to be able to communicate.

Book Review Excerpts

You should be asking for book reviews before you launch the book. When you get them, choose excerpts from the best ones and compile them onto a sheet along with basic information about the book. The best outcome would be to have a journalist write about you, prompting others to buy your book and maybe even write a review. You can spring for a Kirkus Review. The costs vary but are respected industry-wide. They tell you up front you may not like what they say. However, if they do love your book, then the review is gold.

Photos

Include links to high-resolution headshots and a few environmental shots that show you in a variety of settings. For example, a cookbook might include photos of the author in the kitchen, whipping up a favorite dish, or shopping at a local farmer's market. Pamela Fagan Hutchins sent me a picture of her writing outside with her horses. I loved it so much I included it in the interview. Small newspapers, newsletters, and bloggers will welcome these photos. You will also need a photo of your book cover.

Caution: Update your headshot every couple of years. Several years ago, I helped out at a conference where we had invited several well-known authors. I kept looking for one in particular. When I discovered I'd been talking to her earlier I nearly fell over. The picture on all her books must have been taken twenty years earlier. She also didn't bother to dress up or wear makeup. Part of me felt let down. Be professional.

Amazon

1. **Author Central** – You need to do this. It is free and very helpful to the new or established author. This is where you post your biography, photos, blog, video, and events which goes to your author page on Amazon.com

2. **Amazon Scout** – A reader-powered publishing tool for Kindle. It's a place where readers help decide if a book gets published. It's a nice way to get a contract with Amazon.

3. **Kindle World** - http://kindleworlds.amazon.com/faqs?topicid=AAS44RXD0GKNH This model lets the writer create stories based on favorite books, movies, games, etc. You do have to be 18 years or older with a valid U.S. bank account and social security number.

4. **Rankings** – As a reader, I don't pay much attention to ranking. As an author, I'm obsessed with it. https://chrismcmullen.wordpress.com/2014/10/18amazon-com-sales-rank-how-does-it-work-research-bases/ is a nice article explaining how it works. Please note Amazon changes things up whenever they please so the article may not have all the information you require. I like to see my

numbers drop. How do I make them go
down?

- Facebook groups

- Promotions

- Social Media Blitz

- Giveaways

- Blog/Interviews

5. **Free Days** – Getting the biggest bang for
   your bucks

   - Plan ahead – schedule your free reduced
     book about two weeks ahead

   - A week before the event find all the free
     outlets that will post your book on the
     days you've scheduled the event. Some
     of these ask that you sign up a couple of
     weeks ahead of time and others, just a
     few days. You may need to sign up for
     notifications too.

   - Don't forget to use Twitter. They have a
     number of groups in your genre where
     you can post your novel for free.

- Write some clever social media quips to use along
  with your Amazon link. Post one of your Canva
  creations too on all of your Facebook groups. Here
  are a few I've used with success.

Other Amazon Helpful Hints

- **KDP** – This Pint-on-demand company is only one of the tools authors can use to publish their work online. They offer several ways to get noticed after you download your book to their service. Kindle Select is one of those ways to reach a larger audience. You can also have five days each ninety-day period where you can offer your book for free. (I mentioned this earlier.) Why offer it for free? To get noticed by readers who might not otherwise give you a second glance. By doing this you may just get fans for the next book. Besides, you only need to do it one day and you'll see your stats or ranking improve dramatically.

- **Other Options:** There are many print on demand companies. You don't have to go with Kindle Direct Publishing, (KDP) which is an Amazon sister company. If KDP doesn't suit your needs, try IngramSpark, Draft 2 Digital, LuLu, Kobo or Smashwords. Your best recourses are other indie authors. Ask who they recommend and what are the pros and cons of that company.

- **ACX** – Need a finished audiobook? This is one of the places now available for authors. ACX has become a marketplace where you can connect with narrators, engineers, and recording studios, which can see your product to the end. There are various ways of payment and royalties so be sure you read the contract before signing on the dotted line. Everyone I know who has created an audiobook has been very pleased with the experience. They aren't the only company out there so look around.

- **Amazon Marketing Services** – Advertise your book by using Pay-Per-Click ads. You can establish a daily budget and be in control all along the way.

- **Author Tools and Services** – This page offers so much information on how to market your book I'm not even going to try and explain it. Here is the link: amazonauthorinsights.com/tools-and-service

6. **Reviews** – Be careful what you wish for. Book reviews have impact how your book is perceived, but without them it can potentially put your book in a state of limbo. A positive review, will impact your next reader and encourages them to try other books you've written. And yes, there are bad reviews. Having said that, if you

have all good reviews Amazon tends to think you might be buying or gifting something to get them. An occasional less than stellar review might work in your favor.

It is possible that some people don't understand how to write a review. I've included a sheet you can send them to explain. This is only an example. You'll want to make it your own and add something personal.

How to Write & Publish Book Reviews for Authors

Authors LOVE book reviews. Not only do they encourage new readers to buy and try our offerings, but book reviews help author rankings on e-book retailer sites. The more buzz-reviews, stars, likes, etc.—the higher the rankings. When people are talking about our books, good things happen.

Personally, I won't review a book I found bad or just didn't like. It feels too mean to me and falls into the category of, "If you don't have anything nice to say…". If you read and like my book, GREAT. I'm excited. If you read and DON'T like my book, I understand. We can still be friends.

I am not asking you to write a false or fake review for myself or any author. You do what feels right. One thing you might want to avoid, however, is mentioning anything along the lines of "my friend Tierney…". While true, it might give folks the wrong impression and discredit your review.

Some tips for reviewing from Writers Write here. Check it out before you write your reviews if have questions. http://writerswrite.co.za/how-to-write-a-great-books-review.

Reviews fall into the categories of Comment and Opinion. They are also grouped with Columns and Humor.

When writing a review, you are expressing your opinion. Remember to be fair. You can be witty, but you should never be nasty. (I can't imagine any of you being that way.)

Your reviews on Goodreads, Nook, blogs, etc. are all appreciated as well. In the meantime, here is a guide for Amazon. I'm sure you've already done this but thought I'd include it anyway.

Posting a Review on Amazon.com

Amazon.com – Most of my book sales (as well as your other favorite authors' sales) will likely come from Amazon. It's THE place for books.

1. Go to www.amazon.com

2. Sign in or create a new account if you don't already have an Amazon account. You probably already use one.

3. Search for the book you want to review. In this case, it will be **The Rescued Heart by Tierney James.**

4. Click on customer reviews to the right of the STARS.

5. Select Write a Review

6. Click on the book you wish to review and highlight the number of stars. The more stars the better.

7. A box will then appear for you to write and submit your review. It might take twenty-four hours to appear.

Why Blogging Is Important for Authors

Some authors groan at the thought of developing a long-term online marketing strategy for their books because it's yet another demand on their time. (Time they'd like to spend writing.) Extra time isn't something any of us have in ample supply, so I totally understand. This is why I tell authors to select a few things that matter most to build their community and brand. For book authors in a competitive marketplace, the need to blog couldn't be higher. I understand social media continues to evolve, but blogging should remain a top priority for authors.

Let's take a closer look at some of the compelling reasons why you, as an author, need to blog.

Blogging your way to success. Remember the movie *Fields of Dreams*? The catch phrase that many of us still use was, "If you build it, they will come." Blogs are your Field of Dreams. But you have to build it if you want people to come. If you are like me, I don't want people to think I have a little hobby I play with every day. It's the business of writing. If I don't write I'll go out of business pretty quickly. If I open up a used clothing store and never tell people about my amazing selection of vintage clothing and jewelry, no one will come to try out the store. Market the heck out of your blog.

Blogging defines your audience. Find readers who are interested in what you write about. The regular practice of blogging helps you discover the perfect audience you want to reach and the community you want to build.

Use your blog to build interest and anticipation. Build curiosity and expectation for your book with your blog by using some of the research you squirreled away. Maybe your setting is in Iceland. I bet a lot of people would like to know why Iceland? Why go there? Think of your blog as a content tease for your book. Put a link to your Pinterest board on Iceland.

Showcase your value. Let your readers sample your content and use your knowledge base to solve problems for your audience. Afraid to travel abroad? Have a security expert give some travel tips. What about authors in other countries? They know exactly what you should be looking out for when traveling.

Don't be stinky! Keep it fresh. You wouldn't wear the same socks all week, or heaven forbid, the same underware. Think of the kinds of content which you find most useful for you. Then develop ideas, articles, pictures, and interviews to support that love. I interview authors, do book reviews, marketing, travel tips and personal stories for my blog. I also use my research to spin something interesting.

Be an expert. Blogging transforms you into an authority on your subject matter. I was a geography teacher and I love cultures. It is a great way to share my knowledge. Sometimes when you test the waters it is only lukewarm. Keep trying. I know lots of authors and no one can agree on how often you need to blog. Consistency seems to be the key to part of the success. Don't promise your readers a weekly recipe then fail to deliver. However many times you decide to post, keep it going.

Promotion baby! Fauzie Burke, author of _Online Marketing for Busy Authors, says:_ "Blogs provide you with the opportunity to link your content to your books, eBooks, whitepapers, audio recordings, slide presentations, videos and webinars. This provides a number of cross-promotional opportunities. You might even catch the attention of the Today Show or featured in USA Today." Dream big! Follow Fauzia Burke on Twitter: www.twitter.com/FauziaBurke She has lots of good advice.

You can build your digital reputation. Your blog shows up on Amazon, search engines and other websites, which helps to create your reputation.

Branding with a blog. Every blog you write helps define your personal brand. I'll admit creating your personal brand takes time, and fortunately the tools are free and you are already a skilled writer. When you become known as an expert in a field you also become more valuable to publishers and agents.

Worthwhile organizations and institutions may invite you to be a keynote speaker to an audience because of your witty, yet informative blog. You will be positioning yourself to promote more books, apps, conferences, videos, public speaking, your website, and more. Make this a part of your weekly brand management. When you're writing your list of things to do for the week, put it right above daily flossing. It's important too.

Purposes of Blogging. One of the things I do is offer my blog for other authors to strut their stuff. They will drive traffic to your website and blog from their base. You instantly have new eyes on your site. It might just get you some new followers, and email addresses for your blog and newsletter.

Reputation is Everything. Blogging makes you searchable and findable. You're building a reputation as someone "in the know."

Write A book. Yes, creating your next book is not as easy as stringing together a collection of your blogs, but it's much easier to write a 500 to 1,000-word blog than it is to type out a 70,000-word book. Those big projects are more easily accomplished in small bites. Andy Weir, the author of The Martian, started his #1 bestseller as a blog. Never in his wildest dreams did he think it would turn into a book then a blockbuster movie. The book you are reading now, started out as a series of blogs and workshop presentations.

How often to blog? Be consistent! I know I keep saying this over and over. The answer is: every week or once a month. Readers need to know they can count on you. I try to write a series of blogs concerning whatever my work-in-progress (WIP) involves. I save them in a document and to my flash drive with the manuscript. I also include interviews and social media blasts I want to use upon launching the book. Another trick is I try to choose one day (Sunday) I'm not so busy. I'll get the blog ready and post in the evening or have it ready for Monday. Makes things simple.

How to start a blog?

Choose a platform (WordPress, Blogger, etc.)

Choose a focus:

1. What are you passionate about and can write forever concerning the topic?
2. What other kinds of writing do you do that can tie in?
3. What do you hope to accomplish with your blog?
4. Will the blog be personal or topical?

What makes a great content/blog?

1. Title –Make it catchy

2. Opener draws people in

3. Main points that people might care about

4. Give a take away (how will your life be different by reading this?)

Types of blog posts:

1. Top 10 Reasons

2. Tips (how to be a great cook)

3. How to do or become something trending

4. Pep talk/Motivational story with a message

5. Research

6. Response to something going on in the news (be careful)

7. Rant (be careful here too!)

8. Pre-Sale or contest

9. Series

Tips on blogging

1. Be consistent (Sorry. I had to say it again.)

2. Frequency (once a week or once a month)

3. Not too long or short. 600 words is a good number

4. Colorful and sharp format appearance

5. Headlines

6. Connect your blog on social media

7. Be a guest on other blogs and add your blog to the interview

8. Linking to other famous bloggers like Publicity Hound, is a good way to get noticed.

Topics for blogging when your brain drains

- Christmas gifts for authors, kids, teachers, seniors, married children, neighbor

- Travel tips, ideas, destinations

- Safety

- Summer fun

- Bullies

- Bad boys we hate to love

- Why guys love naughty girls

- Gardening tips

- Education

- Sewing

- Hobbies

- Shopping

- Best coffee shops

- Favorite books

- Best movies

- Your office or offices of people you know

- Home tours

- Cultural awareness

- Things to do at the library

- Why children need to love reading before they can read

- Food and cooking tips

- Pets

- Caring for aging parents

- Faith

- Holiday Fun

- Holiday recipes

- Interviews

- Car restoration

- Art

- Fashion and makeup

- Worthy Causes

- Homeopathic medicine

- Memoirs

- Historical sites

- Music

- Dance

- Book reviews

- Tips on organization

- Getting to know your neighbors

- Home decorating

- Sports

- Know your state

- Staying young

- Staying fit

- Political commentary

- Write a story

- Antiques – Your own Roadshow

- Life on the water

- Life in the mountains

- Life after death

- Life after retirement

- Life without children
- Life with children
- Life with stepchildren
- Life after divorce
- Adoption
- Marketing
- Business Opportunities
- Investment
- How to be a_____
- Pitfalls of _____
- Adventures of a lifetime
- Dos and don'ts of _____
- Famous people from your state or community
- First aid
- Careers
- Living off the grid
- Weddings
- Addiction
- Crime
- Being single

- Women (or men) of distinction

Marketing & Time Management Tools

Kind of like running with the bulls. You're terrified, anxious, optimistic and then all these marketing ideas come charging toward you! So, you find the nearest way out and are safe again. But what if you really could run with the bulls? What if you made it the whole way without getting shish kabobbed by an angry bull or in this case a book launch.

1. Book Funnel https://bookfunnel.com/

2. BookBub
   https://www.bookbub.com/welcome

3. Facebook Ads

4. Book Daily http://www.bookdaily.com/

5. Books   Butterfly
   http://www.booksbutterfly.com

6. Fiverr https://www.fiverr.com/

7. Galley Cat www.adweek.com/galleycat/15-places-to-promote-your-book-for-free/77298

Basically, for your Google search write "best places to market my book" in your search bar. Some will have a small charge and others may not. Try the free ones first. Authors don't have a lot of money to spend on marketing so every penny counts.

Time to Change

I write full time these days. When I gave up my day job, I believed I could produce three or four novels a year, write several blogs a week, get on the speakers' tour and still have time to keep up the laundry. I envisioned my home on Pinterest, full of chic ideas and dreamy gardens. Well, the laundry still piles up and I'm lucky if I get one or two novels out a year. There are still dust bunnies under the bed and eating over the sink is easier than cooking some days. Fortunately, my kids have their own homes now so I don't fear I'll get hot lined for neglect.

I went through a phase where I couldn't believe I ever had time to work outside the home. (Notice I said outside the home! We all know being at home is a full-time job.) I began to list things which interfered with writing. Turns out a few simple adjustments helped me stay on track. Remember; you must keep writing no matter what. To keep your name out there, you're going to have to get used to producing words that matter. Here are a few time management ideas to help you stay on track.

- **Turn off Distractions** – Social media is a dark hole. Set a timer for how long you allow yourself to be on Facebook, Twitter, etc. Do it first thing in the morning then after dinner. Keep your phone handy in case the school calls about a sick child or family member is in need of help. Family first.

- **Timer** – Decide on a chunk of time you'll write. Thirty minutes. An hour. Two hours. Whatever it is, stick to it. Make it a habit. Set your timer and write.

- **Take Breaks** – I need coffee so I get up every hour or so and fix me a hot brew. Warming my hands on the side of the cup actually makes me think clearer and I feel refreshed. While I'm up I'll throw those wet clothes into the dryer and start another load. Next time I'll take something out for dinner to thaw or throw in the Crock Pot. Take a walk. Go through the mail. Call your mom. Sit on the front porch with the dog. Now get back to work. Your twenty-minute break is over.

- **Goals are Gold** – Set goals for your day. Will you write two pages, a thousand words, a chapter, an outline or write queries to a potential publisher? Put these down in your planner so you hold yourself accountable. Your journey starts with small steps.

- **Other Writers** – Writing buddies can help you stay on track. I have a couple who call or email me to make sure I'm not surfing the internet or catching up on Outlander. I do the same for them.

- **Rewards** – Do you celebrate your successes? Decide if it will it be a daily, a weekly or at project completion? Do whatever keeps you writing.

- **Change of Geography** – Move the laptop to the couch, outside on the porch, your bed, anywhere to get the stiffness out of your back and legs. A new location could be just the jumpstart you need. Maybe your significant other springs for a hotel for a few days. I once wrote a big chunk of a book at a boutique hotel in St. Louis. The staff pampered me because they knew I was a writer. Maybe this falls under rewards. The time alone really cleared my head.

- **Help Wanted** – I've never been able to do this because I tend to want to clean for the cleaning lady or think my children should be able to pick up after themselves. Now I feel I can finally afford some help even though I really can handle things myself. But this is another area where you could carve out some time for yourself if these busy chores clutter up your head and energy. Decide what is needed. How much it will cost. Can family members take these on for rewards or allowances?

Webinars

Are they worth your time? How expensive are they? What should I expect? All of these are good questions to consider when you feel you need to step it up a bit concerning your marketing strategy. In one of my blog posts, I talk about getting started by reading a number of books I've used in my journey to book promotion. But maybe you are more of an auditory learner and need that voice along with a slideshow to really hammer things home. I get it. I have a pretty short attention span so variety is the spice of life for me too.

Are they worth your time? The short answer is "YES"! Most of these webinars are only about an hour long. You sign up on your computer. I get emails from several sources; The Publicity Hound's Joan Stewart, Chandler Holt, Wesley Atkins and Mark Dawson have their own methods or invite successful promoters to give a quick "how-to" webinar that gives you information in small bites. (Remember I like it short and sweet!)

When I get one of these invites the first thing I want to know is when it will be held. Because I'm a full-time author, my time is much more manageable than most. However, there are times I forget or actually do have an appointment. Most of the time there is a replay later in the day if you've signed up ahead of time. That works for me.

- **How expensive are they?** Although there is a cost for some of these webinars, I only sign up for the free ones. Just like most authors, my money is stretched pretty tight, so I use those dollars wisely. The free ones are packed with useful information. Admit it! Your brain can only store so much data so you might as well grab the free stuff. Almost all the ones I've participated in have a special deal at the end for templates, promotional materials, books (some are free if you sign up for a newsletter) or publicity ideas. Most of the time I don't do these but sometimes I do. The Publicity Hound is a great website to subscribe to and the webinars are fun. Joan is very generous and she has helped me with a number of speed bumps. She even offered to give me a free fifteen-minute consolation, which of course I accepted. The saying, "You get what you pay for," isn't true in this case. FREE really is better.

- **What should you expect?** That really depends on the topic and the instructor. There are a few people I know won't let me down whether it is their webinar or someone they've invited to teach. I never hesitate to join in their programs. You'll need a computer and mute the sound so your yapping dog chasing the cat won't interrupt the group. A link will be sent to your email so you can log in a few minutes before the webinar begins. You'll even get a reminder. Ok, I'll admit a few times I've forgotten all about what I've signed up for because I'm writing fast and furious to get my characters out of a dangerous life or death situation. I need the reminder!

- **Presentation.** A slideshow is the usual method I've enjoyed. They move along slow enough you can take notes. Keep in mind there is a possibility they will offer the printout at the end, so listen for those instructions. I like this because I can crank up the sound and fold a load of towels, start dinner or just prop my feet up on the couch for an hour while I listen to the presenter. I've learned some pretty clever tricks from these guys. Some of which I've messed up big time and others I'm still trying to get the hang of. Since I didn't pay anything for the training, I'm not out any money. I keep those notes in a notebook to refer to later when I need them. This is really easy. Don't hesitate.

Marketing doesn't have to be tedious or scary. You can do this. Keep being awesome.

People to Follow

Joanna Penn https://www.thecreativepenn.com/

Wesley Atkins http://www.kdspy.com/

Joan Stewart – The Publicity Hound
https://publicityhound.com/

Tierney James – The Write Stuff
https://www.pinterest.com/ptierneyjames/the-write-stuff-with-tierney-james/

Getting Noticed

Unless you have a star on Hollywood's Walk of Fame or have received a nomination for Best Screenplay at the Academy Awards, you probably are looking for ways to get noticed. I often wonder how I can get myself on PBS News Hour to showcase my book. You have to start somewhere so here are some suggestions.

1. Book signings

2. Conferences

3. Public speaking

4. Book clubs

5. Interviews

6. Submit books & products to the new product review section of local newspapers, magazines & trade publications.

7. Form alliances with groups that are in a good position to help you sell your book. They may have a related product, service or cause. Donate a book, offer to give a workshop.

8. Host other authors on your event page, blog, etc.

9. Submit a "How to article" that ties in with the theme of your next book.

10. Make photos current & professional.

11. Publish everywhere you can or have the energy to produce.

12. Publish white papers – White papers is an industry report on something that is cutting edge in the news today. Research a topic like the Zika Virus in your area or in new mothers. Crime in your town. Victims of (whatever) is your theme.

13. Create a product that goes with your book or topic. My bookmarks for Dance of the Devil's Trill and KitKats (my main character's name was Kat) were a hit. Lipstick samples for my business cards LIPSTICK & DANGER, Recipe booklets or other brochures that go with your book. My character Tessa makes wonderful chocolate chip cookies. I've offered the recipe with some success.

14. Follow-up with a thank you note to those who host, interview or mentioned you in an article.

15. Capture email addresses - https://www.campaignmonitor.com/blog/email-marketing/2015/05/capture-email-address-website/

16. Facebook Fan Page

17. Leave business cards wherever you go (even the library).

18. Grand opening events that tie in with your theme.

19. Join community groups like Chamber of Commerce and Garden Club.

20. Promote other writers by sharing on social media.

21. Let readers name a character.

22. Contests for book giveaways.

23. Speaker for women's and civic groups.

24. Women's expo

25. Men's expo

26. County fairs

27. Wear promotional materials or give tee shirts to friends to wear.

28. Bumper sticker for your website.

29. Donate your book to libraries, schools and military programs for soldiers abroad.

30. High school reunions

31. Volunteer at writers' conferences.

32. Spring and fall festivals

33. Mentor for aspiring writers

34. Relaunch a not-so-new book with new book cover and special event.

35. Be a guest speaker for your child's school during some special event like careers, write-a-thon or Read Across America which happens in February.

36. Panelist for a writers' conference.

37. Visit an event for free but ask to be able to sell your books.

38. College alumni newsletters

39. Keep social media up to date.

40. State school conventions often want workshop ideas or guest speakers.

Creating the Notebook

This is not the Nicholas Sparks book or movie. After today, start creating your marketing notebook. Decide on the categories you want to include. I'm sure you'll have some that I do not. There is no right or wrong way unless you decide not to do one at all. Trust me you'll forget some ideas and wish you knew where you put them.

Categories:

- Street Team
- Marketing

- Media Kit

- Resources

- Launch party info

- Venues to visit - past and future

- Book Reviewers

- How to write review instructions – I give these to my reviewers.

- Personal biography

- Social media plan

- Publishers

- Blogging basic

- Promo, flyers, brochures

- Branding possibilities

- Swag

- Your book blurbs

- Press releases

- Business cards shared

- Copies of articles, awards, and interviews

- Business plan

- Cost of doing business worksheet – It is also good to have during tax season.

- Other

There are books that say 10 minutes a day or an hour a day is enough. It depends on you and what you are dealing with your daily activities and schedule. Sitting on the couch watching NCIS and the hunky Gibbs isn't going to get much done. I'm not saying don't watch it. (I never miss it!) Just don't make it an excuse. Carve out time each day to do something to promote yourself and stick in the notebook. Here are some easy things to do while watching NCIS:

Email a thank you note

Post a blog

Interview another author or person in your community – write the questions for you or the author.

Post on Twitter & Facebook groups

Flip through a magazine for ideas

Post a picture on Instagram

Write some social media blurbs

Make two Canva.com memes each night

Only you know if every day or once a week will work. The important thing is to always do something. If you're just now starting out you are ahead of the game.

Reinvent yourself. Be the next Nora Roberts or Vince Flynn.

Should a Writer Create a Business Plan?

The short answer is "heck yes!" The long answer is a little more involved. For a while now, I've set goals for myself, but never really felt bound to it in any way. I kept lists of things I read or money spent on my projects in hopes of using it for a tax deduction.

Last year I took it a little more seriously because I started writing down exactly what I had done for 2016 and honestly, I was a little disappointed. Part of that lack of success (although I made some serious money) was because my parents needed some care. I lived three hours away so a great deal of travel became part of my life. Then my father passed away in September and there tended to be a lot going on with my mother until the spring of 2017. Things continued at a snail's pace with the birth of twins to my daughter. I wanted to be there for her so my writing suffered. It was a trade-off I'm glad I made. Then over Thanksgiving, my mother passed away.

I tell you this because life just happens. Unexpected events are roadblocks to get you off track. Having a plan in place helps me refocus what I want to accomplish. Now my goal/plan I wrote down for 2017 looks like it has bullet holes in it. I'm not sure even the Navy SEALS could rescue it. But I did get some things done. I never gave up. This year my business plan generates excitement in me. I've already tried to implement it so I'm used to the work schedule. My plan will look different than yours.

This is to be broken down into bite-size pieces. Purchase a calendar, a little larger than the size of a spiral notebook. Take your plan and break it up by months or weeks on what you intend to accomplish. In my calendar, I have the month where I put in the basic activity. Then the next few pages have a longer space for each day where I can go into detail. I've padded things in because there is no way I can get everything done. But you never know!

These are my categories. Under each one, I list exactly what I want.

Books to Write

1. Words to write each day (I write these on my calendar to help me keep track.)

2. Number of projects to write (include the title if you know. I always have an idea.)

Marketing

1. Social Media you want to use

2. Ads you want to try

3. Do you need a newsletter?

4. Helping others with promotion

5. Any changes to current published work

Blogging

1. Decide on a number of posts a week/month and stick to it.

2. Decide on the topics you'll cover

3. Write your posts ahead of time

Conference

I like this because I can start saving for the event. But you need to start scouting out where and what you want to do now. Just because you add them to the plan doesn't mean you have to go. These are the ones I'm interested in this year. More on this later.

Possible Places

- Killer Nashville

- Bouchercon

- Between the Pages Writers Con

- Ozark Creative Writers

Possible Speaking Appearances

I hesitate to show you my list because I want you to find what works for your topic, expertise and comfort zone. Here are a few ideas that might work for you. Remember if your character has a garden or is a farmer you might contact the local garden club, etc.

1. Workshops – marketing & writing

2. Women's groups at churches or conferences

3. Book clubs

4. Community groups like Rotary, Lions Club, Chamber of Commerce

Growth

I really go off the rails here. Trying to work this into our hectic schedules, tends to be difficult for me. Knowing I've written it down and committed to closing the computer for a few hours helps me tremendously.

1. Read two books a month in my genre

2. Take one free seminar a month

3. Read one educational advice book on writing a month

4. Read devotional/inspirational passage each day

5. Watch two documentaries each month

6. Read one book/magazine/article out of my genre each month (Keep track of the titles.)

7. Read informative magazines each month (List your preference and keep track of them as well.)

8. Meet with other writers for encouragement.

Document in Your Calendar – Be sure you also print off a copy of your plan to place in your calendar where you'll check it each week. Okay! You're ready to start 2018. Go!

Editors Are Your Best Friends

Or as I like to call it - Indiana Jones and the Golden Editor.

Do you remember that first scene in the movie Raiders of the Lost Ark? Indiana Jones carefully maneuvers through a cavern full of spiders, booby-traps, a disloyal guide, and numerous warnings along the way to be careful. Then the golden statue is finally in the hands of the handsome Indiana, only to have it snatched away by yet more pitfalls, natives with spears, and an unscrupulous treasure hunter. My heart races remembering this story.

Writing is exactly like Raiders of the Lost Ark. There lies your manuscript upon the alter of magical tales, beautiful and full of golden words for the taking. The only thing it needs is an editor. If you are an indie author it is up to you to manage the edits somehow. Will you, like the disloyal guide, grab the prize and run with it only to find yourself pinned against the wall with no hope of survival? Or will you be like Indiana Jones and do what it takes to survive? Indiana Jones must have been an indie writer (Get it? *Indi*ana Jones) at heart.

When I first started writing in hopes of landing a contract with a traditional publisher, I worked hard trying to improve my story. I hired someone who did indeed help me make the changes the manuscript needed. Although she wasn't an official editor by trade, her keen eye and intuition guided me enough to make the necessary changes. Sadly, it still wasn't enough. Of course, I didn't know all the ins and outs of editing until I actually got a contract and experienced the gut-wrenching work laid before me once they sent in their editorial raptors. However, I learned many valuable lessons. I became a much better writer. After all, it wasn't personal, just good business.

Then came the day I discovered being an indie author was pretty magical and adventurous. I still wanted the golden prize of success but needed help. So here are some of the things I learned along the way to finding a good editor.

The Do's of Finding an Editor

1. I ask other authors who they use. First, I check out their books to see if the editor has done a good job. I also ask around at writers' conferences.

2. Contact several editors and tell them about your project.

3. Are they sensitive to your concerns?

4. Do they answer your questions in a timely fashion?

5. Are they upfront about the cost? Ask if they don't tell you.

6. Do they offer other services like formatting, cover design and help with promotion?

7. How long can you expect them to take with your manuscript?

8. How in depth are their edits?

9. Do you have to alert them ahead of time to be put in the queue? If so how much in advance? This makes a difference if you are on a deadline, which I often am.

10. Be kind, respectful, friendly and polite. Be a professional. I've never met my editor in person, but we have visited on the phone and by email. We've developed a friendship where both of us feel comfortable in sharing our lives with each other. That makes it a whole lot easier when you get your edits back and it looks like someone opened a vein over the pages.

The Don'ts of Finding an Editor

1. Using friends and family members can cause hurt feelings if they tell you the truth. More than likely they won't, which is even worse because then you have a manuscript that even the disloyal guide in Raiders of the Lost Ark wouldn't touch. It's okay for them to read over it, but not be your editor.

2. Don't take the first one that comes along. You want to get references, read their work, see if there have been complaints.

3. Don't be demanding or be that writer who thinks their words are golden. They aren't. If an editor suspects you're difficult to work with, you won't make it across that chasm when you leap across like Indiana. That door will close and you'll be left high and dry.

4. Don't refuse to make changes. If this is something you find difficult then before signing on with an editor ask if they might edit a sample chapter to see how they work, their style, and if together, you are able to see a mutual vision for the project. You want someone who will listen to your concerns, but by shutting them out you've wasted time—mostly theirs, not to mention money.

5. Don't negotiate the fee. You already know how hard it is to make money as an author. They are making your baby golden so in the end, it has worth.

6. Don't send an editor something that is poorly researched. It makes their job harder and they really don't have time to do that for you. Not being on your game is a quick way to lose a good editor.

7. If you are a first-time author in search of an editor, be willing to open yourself up to change. Don't keep making the same mistakes over and over. It is frustrating to an editor and they may question whether the two of you are a good fit.

8. Don't send an editor an unpolished manuscript you haven't bothered to edit or have someone take a look at first. My last manuscript I sent to several readers and they found some problems with the storyline. There were unanswered questions never addressed. I went back to fix those potholes before I sent it to the editor. Even though there were still things I needed to do, I felt confident my editor wouldn't throw up in a nearby trashcan.

Attending A Conference Is Good Marketing

After starting my first novel, I decided I needed to go to a writer's conference almost five hours from home. I chose the Oklahoma Writers' Conference Inc. https://www.owfi.org/conference2018/ One of the deciding factors was Steve Berry would be the keynote speaker. Since I was a huge fan, I didn't want to miss it. My friends feared I'd be arrested for stalking my author hero. When he passed me in the hall and saw that I was carrying his latest book, Mr. Berry stopped and offered to sign it for me. I slipped in my own drool and could only manage to give a pitiful nod. Apparently, I developed a momentary stutter.

To think I almost chickened out and stayed home! While there, I went to so many workshops and met informative speakers who once stood at the starting line just like me. To my surprise, there were no strangers; everyone had a story to tell and wanted to know more about me. When I left three days later, a fire of determination burned in my belly. I wanted to complete this journey. I give the OWFI credit for giving me the confidence to keep going.

I attended two more conferences after that; one was very small but packed with helpful information. Because it was only a thirty-minute drive and a one-day conference, I could manage the cost. I even got to practice pitching my book to an agent. Nothing came of it but the experience was sweet, encouraging and helpful. The conference I attended a few weeks later, although good, had a New York City agent with the sensitivity of a black mamba and no idea how new writers felt about sharing their ideas. She killed me.

Remember that high school English teacher that didn't like my work? This agent made her look like Florence Nightingale. She basically told me no one cared what I wrote. Truth. By this time, I had two other conferences under my belt, and knew that just wasn't true. However, I made a couple of great friends who became writing buddies and experienced the same thing when they pitched to her. Not everyone will like what you write. REMEMBER THAT!!! It's okay. You aren't going to like every agent, publisher or reader either. That's life.

So why attend a conference if you are going to get smacked around. Since that time, I've been to a lot of writing conferences. All of them have been wonderful, friendly and encouraging. Besides a good cup of coffee, my drug of choice is a writers' conference. I just can't help myself. I come away so pumped. Here is a list of reasons to consider and how it can help you in your marketing journey.

1. Meet other writers, authors, agents, publishers.

2. Discover helpful lessons in improving your work in progress.

3. Learn how to become an indie author and gain tools you'll need.

4. Practical workshops.

5. Come away inspired, motivated and with a stronger belief in yourself.

6. Enter a writing contest. Most of these conferences have one.

7. Explore other genres you might want to write.

8. Discover that in all walks of life, someone you know wants to be a writer. I was a teacher. One of my instructors at the conference was a lawyer. At another conference, the instructor was a former FBI agent. You never know who you'll meet and how their journey led them to you if you don't go.

9. Take advantage of pitching your manuscript. You might land an agent or a contract.

10. Networking. I now have friends across the country and on several continents, who support me when I release a new book. That came from being at a writer's conference.

Remember how I stuttered and drooled when I met Steve Berry? Since that time, I've come out of my shell and don't lose my cool when I meet big-time authors. In many settings, like Killer Nashville, all you have to do is invite one of these keynote speakers to come sit at your table and they gladly join you and your new friends. Remember. We as writers tend to be solitary creatures so we stay hunkered over our computers instead of having dinner with friends or some other normal activity. Those keynote speakers want you to invite them to your table.

Resource Management

Let's take a breath here. When I started out there wasn't anyone to tell me what to do. I often wonder if I'd be in a different place had I researched all the things I'm telling you. Yes, I knew I needed to market myself, but I was clueless what that really meant. Now I know. For every hour I write I plan on several more hours setting up marketing procedures, collecting data on my project and searching for interesting tidbits to offer my readers.

There is a saying: "It takes five years to be an overnight success." I have to wonder if that is because most of us are stumbling around in the dark pitching our crafts, ideas, and books. I'm four years in and I'm starting to see the light at the end of the tunnel.

I thought if I read all the books on writing, and I have tons, everything would just fall into place. Nope. Here are some of the books I can recommend for you to use as a guide. Some are free eBooks and others I purchased because I wanted to scribble on each page or be unplugged for a while.

Books to read – There are many more, but these are the ones I have on my Kindle.

Guerrilla Marketing for Writers by Jay Conrad Levinson, Rick Frishman, Michael Larsen & David L. Handcock.

How to Market a Book by Joanna Penn

5-Minute Marketing for Authors by Barb Asselin

30 Day Book Marketing Challenge by Rachel Thompson

How to Market & Sell Your Book over the Holidays by Frankie Johns

How to Launch Your E-Book by Mimi Emmanuel

Book Launch by Chandler Bolt

How to Get a Truckload of Reviews on Amazon.com by Penny Sansevieri

Websites & links to promote yourself – There are many more!

http://shaebaxter.com/public-domain-images/
LOTS of stock photos with no copyright restrictions

7 Ways to Use the Best Free Media Database for Publicity.
http://publicityhound.com/blog/usnplhttp://www.usnpl.com/Best Book Promotion Site - Author Marketing Experts

Adwww.amarketingexpert.com/sellmorebooks

Book Promotion Service - Fiverr.com

Adwww.fiverr.com/eBook-Promotion

List of 100+ Book Promotion Sites & Free Submission Toolwww.readersintheknow.com/list-of-book-promotion-sites

Best Book Promotion Sites 2017 | Paid Author www.paidauthor.com/best-ebook-promotion-sites/

InDtale Magazine <tjmackay@indtale.com> Love this one!

Missouri Library Association – Don't forget to check out their conference schedule

Missouri Association of School Librarians – Conference for 2017 was at Union Station in St. Louis – You can be a vendor. I give a few librarians bookmarks to pass out at their annual conference. Nice to be friends with these folks.

Local newspaper – offer to do an interview

Missouri Libraries
http://libraries.regionaldirectory.us/missouri.htm

Writing Conferences – Offer to give a workshop – You may get your picture and name in the program.

Chamber of Commerce – Your local chamber may like telling everyone they have a writer or author living among the town folk! Be a member.

Bumper Sticker – Advertise your website. I get some looks with LIPSTICK & DANGER written on my bumper.

Penned Con – These are throughout the US but the one I'm familiar with is Penned-Con St. Louis. You meet readers and offer some goodies or swag for them to take home. One of the things I do is tape a lipstick sample to my business card that says Lipstick & Danger.

Street Teams

The definition of a street team is a group of fans who support an artist, band, author or other creative individual. For our purposes let's just discuss what a street team can do for you as an author. The author's street team is responsible for getting the word out about their latest book. They become the ambassadors of your marketing life.

Street Teams are chosen by the author for a variety of reasons:

- Have read your work in the past
- Signed up to read and review your ARC (advanced reader copy)

- Have computer skills which you need

- Love social media

- Possess connections to the community of readers you want to reach

- Dependable, smart and encouraging

- Love being part of something big and new

How many members can join your group? Five is a good number to start with at a minimum. Choose from your friends and family for a base if they are willing. Take into consideration their jobs, health, children, school, and your relationship. Something to remember when choosing family is you don't want someone who feels pressured or obligated to help you. If it becomes a chore, most likely, they won't do a good job.

My Street Team consists of fifteen members. Some of them are more active than others for reasons I've already mentioned. I write a great deal of content in a year's time. The lives of my team members oscillate. I need to be understanding when things go south for them.

From time to time I replace members if they aren't holding up their end. I need them to be a part of my inner circle. A fresh face is always a nice addition. Sometimes people just get tired of being on the front lines. My numbers expand and contract throughout the year.

I created a closed Facebook page where I communicate with my team. We share our lives, updates, and events whenever necessary. This has proven to be an easy and successful means of keeping track of the Street Team who go the extra mile for me.

Here is a sample of my call to action for new Street Team members for Lipstick and Danger. I've also included the guidelines to participate. You'll want to write your own which fits your needs and style.

Street Team Kits

Choose what is best for your people.

- Bookmarks and postcards to distribute
- Amazon or Starbucks card ($5)
- Thank you note for participating
- Swag you use at book signings (keychains, magnets, candy)
- Street Team Rules
- Tee Shirt displaying your book cover.
- Tea bags or gourmet instant coffee packets
- Hand lotion

- List of where to leave bookmarks, etc.

I try to tie the packets to something which goes along with the book. For my book *The Rescued Heart,* I made necklaces or earrings with a heart. *Dance of the Devil's Trill*, I had Etsy make keychains with the book cover and an angel wing dangling on the end. My magnets feature the Enigma Series. Be creative.

STREET TEAM NEEDED

I wanted to ask you about being a permanent part of my street team. You may have been asked before by me on other projects. Since I was feeling my way through social media obligations as mandated by either my publisher or just me, I have begun to see what it takes to mount a campaign for selling books. Without you, my job becomes a great deal more difficult.

If this is the first time you are hearing of a street team let me just give you a brief overview. A street team member supports the author (in this case me) by retweeting, reposting on Facebook and even reading the ARC (advanced reader's copy) of a book about to be released. You are also asked to post a review of the book.

How often do you participate? That depends on you and your social media connections. I've had members in the past that only used one site but used it successfully to get the word out. Sometimes I have book signings for the release of a new book, but more times than not, I have an online party that works for everyone. It's fun and you can do it in your PJs with your favorite beverage. There are times I do a special "HELP!!!" signal. I'll send you a sheet on that later, but it is basically where you earn points for doing a blast of "Hey, have you read…" Don't worry. I can write the tweets and promo for you. All you do is cut and paste. (Unless you want to use your own words.)

I try and send my team members something in the way of appreciation. Sometimes it is Starbucks or Amazon card. Other times it might be a copy of the published book. I try to mix it up..

Maybe you don't want to do each book because of time constraints in your life at a particular time. No problem. Just let me know and I can put you on hold. You'll still be able to be a part of the group set up just for you to see postings, announcements, and events. You can weigh in at any time. The reason I'm reaching out to you is that you've been supportive in the past and I know I can count on you in the future. I will have a special group on Facebook just for us.

In the next two to six months I have two more novels that will be released. *Dance of the Devil's Trill* (paranormal/urban fantasy thriller) and Vol. III of the Enigma Series *Rooftop Angels.* I would love for you to be a part of that. If you are interested please let me know as I begin to set up the private group on Facebook. I will send you a cheat sheet on the details of a street team as well as how to write a review. (Some of you are very good at writing reviews. Thank you!) Although two to six months seems like a long way off I'm probably behind in my preparation for it. Sounds crazy I know!

Thanks in advance for your consideration. Writing is my life. I would love for you to be a part of it.

Tierney James

STREET TEAM RULES & RESPONSIBILITIES

Thanks again for being a part of THE RESCUED HEART STREET TEAM. You will be given the opportunity to get the ARC (advanced reader copy) of this novel. Another benefit to you is that you can earn prizes just for reading, writing reviews and spreading the word about my books and upcoming events.

Team member duties:

- Reading my books and then writing and posting reviews on Amazon, Goodreads, and other sites. I'll send you a document on how to post a review if you've never done it before.

- Tweeting – If I see you mentioning me above and beyond the call of duty by using @TierneyJames1 and #romantic suspense or other appropriate hashtags you may win a special thank you from me.

- Sharing and posting on your Facebook page

- Other creative ways that you devise to spread the word. You'll need to send me links or pics. Your awesomeness and creativity will be so much fun. Some ideas would be taking a picture holding the book with the St. Louis Arch in the background, at a cool restaurant, with a celebrity like Bradley Cooper (I'll pretty much insist on an introduction).

- If you haven't "liked" my author page http://www.facebook/TierneyJamesAction then I would appreciate your attention to that. Takes only a second. Please sign up for my blog, tierneyjames.com/blog as well.

- If you are part of a book club or community group, church, etc. and need a speaker or books for an event, let me know. I will try and assist whenever possible. (Again-that whole Bradley Cooper thing would go a long way.)

Benefits include:

- Author review copies of my new releases

- ARCs of backlisted books on occasion when requested

- Opportunity to win gift certificates to Amazon, Starbucks, and other surprises

- Special prize drawings for gift certificates and other cool swag

- Extra entries in ALL contests I run on my blog

- Awarded a special gift box with swag and promotional materials

DISCLAIMER AND NOTICE OF BEHEADINGS:

By signing up as a member of this team, I am trusting that you will not, under any circumstances, share your copy of my work. Your copy is for YOU ONLY. Any sharing, emailing or posting of content other than what I post myself on my blog, website, etc. is considered PIRACY. My publishers pursue all pirates and crushes them with their sharp swords. Don't be a pirate. Your reply to this email conveys your acceptance of these terms and your desire to be a part of the Lipstick and Danger team. If at any time you wish to be removed from this group or list, please email me, and I'll open your space to another. All terms still apply.

Thank you for believing in me and supporting this journey.

Conclusion

Some people look at life's obstacles and see a kind of contract for defeat. My mother always saw the glass half full, and I want to be just like that as I age. She was legally blind, suffered from a lung disorder and couldn't hear it thunder without her hearing aids. But she would tell me, "I'm just thrilled I can do what I do." My brother and I would laugh and say she was a tough old girl. She grew up dirt poor, had little education and no special training. But she made lemonade out of lemons. I was so proud of her.

This coming year I want to embrace me, the me that likes to sing, write, garden, and hold babies. The thought of traveling to new places, meeting interesting people and reading strange books, tempt me. I want to fill my notebooks with words that inspire my readers to love the life they have and try new things. Will I be on the USA Best Seller List? Maybe! I intend to work toward that and enjoy every minute. The world is a rich environment for writers and I intend to take advantage of opportunities which cross my path.

I hope you'll tag along with me and enjoy the ride. Life is so exciting. We are blessed in this country to explore our options. Don't let yours escape before you can touch them. Be inspired.

I believe with a few marketing jewels in your crown, you'll see success too. Don't give up. Keep trying. Let me know where your journey leads you.

P.S. Don't listen to negative agents, sour English teachers or reviews.

www.ingramcontent.com/pod-product-compliance
Lightning Source LLC
Chambersburg PA
CBHW071023120626
46546CB00003B/1198

* 9 7 8 1 9 6 5 4 6 0 1 6 0 *